Sharing

By Janine Amos   Illustrated by Annabel Spenceley
Consultant Rachael Underwood

Gareth Stevens Publishing
A WORLD ALMANAC EDUCATION GROUP COMPANY

Please visit our web site at: www.garethstevens.com
For a free color catalog describing Gareth Stevens Publishing's
list of high-quality books and multimedia programs,
call 1-800-542-2595 (USA) or 1-800-387-3178 (Canada).
Gareth Stevens Publishing's fax: (414) 332-3567.

Library of Congress Cataloging-in-Publication Data

Amos, Janine.
    Sharing / by Janine Amos; illustrated by Annabel Spenceley.
        p. cm. — (Courteous kids)
    Includes bibliographical references.
    Summary: Provides examples and tips for working things out fairly
when two people want the same thing.
    ISBN 0-8368-3172-1 (lib. bdg.)
    1. Sharing—Juvenile literature. [1. Sharing. 2. Conduct of life.]
I. Spenceley, Annabel, ill. II. Title.
BJ1533.G4A56   2002
177'.1—dc21   2002017717

This edition first published in 2002 by
Gareth Stevens Publishing
A World Almanac Education Group Company
330 West Olive Street, Suite 100
Milwaukee, Wisconsin 53212 USA

Gareth Stevens editor: JoAnn Early Macken
Cover Design: Katherine A. Goedheer

This edition © 2002 by Gareth Stevens, Inc. First published by Cherrytree Press,
a subsidiary of Evans Brothers Limited. © 1997 by Cherrytree (a member of the
Evans Group of Publishers), 2A Portman Mansions, Chiltern Street, London
W1M 1LE, United Kingdom. This U.S. edition published under license from
Evans Brothers Limited. Additional end matter © 2002 by Gareth Stevens, Inc.

Printed in the United States of America

1 2 3 4 5 6 7 8 9 06 05 04 03 02

Note to Parents and Teachers

The questions that appear in **boldface** type can be used to initiate
discussion with your children or class. Encourage them to think of
possible answers before continuing with the story.

Sara and Ali

Ali is playing with all of the dough.

Sara wants to play with dough, too.

Sara grabs the dough away from Ali.

"Hey!" Ali yells.
How does Ali feel?

Dave comes over to talk with Ali and Sara.

"What's going on?" Dave asks.

"I want the dough!" shouts Sara.

"I was using it!" screams Ali.

"You sound angry, Ali," says Dave.

"And, Sara, do you really need
the dough?" he asks.

Ali and Sara both nod.

"I need lots of dough to make my farm," says Ali.

15

"I need some dough to make a pizza," says Sara.

Ali and Sara both want the dough.
What could they do?

17

Sara thinks hard.

"Ali can give me some dough to make my pizza,"
she says, "and he can have the rest."

19

Ali thinks about it.

He gives Sara a handful of dough.
Then he gives her some more.

"You've solved the problem," says Dave.
"You're sharing the dough."

Alexis and Kelly

Alexis has some strawberries.

Kelly comes over.
"I want some strawberries," she says.

"Okay," says Alexis. "Here."

Kelly takes three strawberries.
"That's too many!" says Alexis.

27

How do you think Alexis feels?

What do you think Kelly will do?

Kelly gives Alexis one of her strawberries.

Now Alexis and Kelly each
have two strawberries.

31

Sometimes, two people want the same thing.
If you want something that another person
already has, ask the other person for it.
Talk about what you both need.
Together, you can find a way to share
that will work for both of you.

More Books to Read

It's Mine! Leo Lionni (Dragonfly)

Let's Care About Sharing!
P. K. Hallinan (Hambleton-Hill)

One of Each. Mary Ann Hoberman (Little, Brown)